EXTRAORDINARY CHRISTIANS

Discipleship Ministry Team
Ministry Council
Cumberland Presbyterian Church

September 2015

8207 Traditional Place
Cordova (Memphis), Tennessee 38016

©2015 Discipleship Ministry Team

All Rights Reserved. No part of this book may be reproduced or transmitted in any form or by any means, electronic or mechanical, including photocopying, recording, or by any information storage or retrieval system, without permission in writing from the publisher with the single exception that purchase of this curriculum grants the purchaser the right to copy and distribute student handouts within each lesson for use in their local church. For information address Discipleship Ministry Team, Cumberland Presbyterian Center, 8207 Traditional Place, Cordova (Memphis), Tennessee, 38016-7414.

The Discipleship Ministry Team of the Ministry Council of the Cumberland Presbyterian Church is the successor organization to the Board of Christian Education of the Cumberland Presbyterian Church.

Funded, in part, by your contributions to Our United Outreach.

First Edition 2015

Published by The Discipleship Ministry Team, CPC
Memphis, Tennessee

ISBN-13: 978-0692505908
ISBN-10: 0692505903

We want to hear from you.
Please send your comments about this curriculum to
the Discipleship Ministry Team at faithoutloud@cumberland.org

FAITH OUT LOUD

TEACHING THE LESSON
BY WHITNEY BROWN AND ANDY McCLUNG

SCRIPTURE
PSALM 39:13-16, EPHESIANS 2:22

THEME
Find your niche.

CONECTING TO YOUR STUDENTS

Some teens know exactly what they want to do with their lives. Others have yet to decide. Those who are certain of their future are probably wrong, however, as changing college majors is common, and changing jobs multiple times during one's career is now normal. (Many employers now consider a long tenure a sign of low ambition!) These next few years are a stressful time for teens and young adults. Those with a plan wonder if they're making the right decision or if any positions in their field will be available after graduation. Those without a plan worry that they'll never be able to decide or find the right path in life. Sometimes it can seem futile to make a concrete plan when there are a seemingly infinite amount of options in the world. Adding to this stress may be pushy parents, materialism and greed, or the desire for a career that honors God other than full-time, ordained ministry. Teens need to know the spiritual importance of choosing a good career path.

There is an entire Faith Out Loud lesson on call and vocation. See Volume 1, Quarter 1.

EXPLAINING THE TOPIC

Do a web search for books on the subject of pain, and you'll find titles about managing pain, stopping pain, treating pain, and overcoming pain. But you might notice one that sticks out: The Gift of Pain (formerly titled Pain: The Gift Nobody Wants). The words "pain" and "gift" aren't usually used together. But Dr. Paul Brand thought it made perfect sense.

Paul was British, but born in India in 1914. His father was a medical missionary, but not a doctor. Paul learned the local language, explored the wilds terrain, and saw his parents help the local people in many ways. He remembered three men who were treated differently. His father put on gloves before tending their wounds and made Paul stay away. His mother gave them a basket of food, but forbade Paul from touching it after they left, and Paul's father later burned it. When Paul asked why these men were treated so differently than all the other patients, he learned they were lepers. The word scared him. Nevertheless, he still learned from his parents' example that Christians help those in need.

When Paul was 9, his family returned to England so Paul could attend school. His parents returned to the mission field, leaving Paul with relatives. Paul was smart and creative, but saw no connection between school work and reality. At 16, he quit school and spent five years learning construction, which he intended to use in mission work. He also taught Sunday school and started a youth retreat center. Then, age 21, and unsure of God's call on his life, Paul left construction to take a short, very basic, medical course. He loved it. Now he saw the connection between academics and reality. He attended medical school, intending to become a missionary doctor. Paul was amazed by the human body—especially the hand.

For several years, Paul was distracted from his call by marriage, World War Two, a succession of desirable positions, teaching duties, and a child. But an invitation to lead a hospital back in India restored his mission mindset. While there he found his true calling: helping leprosy patients. Back in, 1947, leprosy was not given much attention by the medical community because of its negative stigma.

It had always been thought that leprosy rotted away the flesh, but Paul discovered that it damages the nerves and thus destroys the sense of touch. Victims can't feel pain so wounds go unnoticed and untreated, then fester and rot. This discovery is why Paul considered pain a gift. God designed the human body to feel pain so we'll know when there's a problem to be taken care of. Paul said most medical complaints—blisters, swelling, fever, coughing, vomiting, and pains—are really symptoms of the body healing itself.

Paul also discovered that leprosy isn't as contagious as most people thought and that besides humans, only armadillos carry the leprosy bacteria! Perhaps his most important realization, though, didn't come from all the medical knowledge in his head, from the Christ-like love for patients in his heart. The spiritually destructive effect of having leprosy is the inability to feel the touch of other humans. Paul says, "Leprosy is a devastatingly lonely disease... of all the gifts we can give a leprosy patient, the one he values most is the gift of being handled and touched."

> Dr. Brand learned early not to use the term "leper" because of the unfairly negative stigma attached to that word.

In India, much like in the Bible and medieval Europe, leprosy victims were sent away from family and home for fear of their disease. Paul Brand's work helped to dispel this stigma. Much of his work on leprosy centered on his fascination with the human hand, what leprosy does to it (damaging the nerves to make it a useless claw), and how to repair some of the damage. He quoted Isaac Newton: "In the absence of any other proof, the thumb alone would convince me of God's existence."

After 19 years in India, Paul came to the U.S. in 1966 to lead the nation's only leprosarium. He came, in part, for access to technology that would improve his work and help it reach the whole world. As technology advanced, though, he never forgot to focus on the patient as a person, loved by God.

After retiring, Paul said that because of his choices of where to work he never made much money. He didn't mind. In fact, he said, "The friends who once were patients bring me more joy than wealth could ever bring.... It's strange—those of us who involve ourselves in places where there is the most suffering, look back in surprise to find that it was there that we discovered the reality of joy."

With Philip Yancey, Paul Brand wrote three books. One of them is titled Fearfully and Wonderfully Made, drawing on Psalm 139:14. In it, Brand marvels at the design of the human body and explores the idea that just as Jesus was God "enfleshed," the Church (as in Christian believers) is now the "dwelling place for God" here on earth (Ephesians 2:22). Dr. Brand died in 2003.

THEOLOGICAL UNDERPINNINGS

The field of medicine is known for its extreme specialization. The Church is not. Back in the 1950s and 1960s, congregations tried to be everything to everybody, and some did a good job of it. But today, better versions of almost everything churches offer are readily available (education, child care, social interaction, recreation, etc.). The things no other entity can offer is what congregations need to focus on today: worship, discipleship, and service in Christ's name. Dr. Brand so wonderfully affected so many lives because he found his niche: treating leprosy patients. Each congregation needs to discern its unique niche, or calling.

In the gospels we see Jesus healing the sick. We Christians are called to be Christ-like, but we can't all be doctors. So we find others ways to help heal—financial donations, supporting medical ministries and missions, voting for candidates with good healthcare reform plans, praying, visiting the sick (much of healing has nothing to do with medicine or treatments), tending to the needs of patients' families (it's easier to focus on getting well when you know your family is taken care of), erasing unfair stigmas attached to certain diseases and disorders (including mental).

When Paul Brand asked his patients and their families who helped most during their suffering, they rarely described someone who had all the answers, or someone who was always upbeat and encouraging. Instead, they almost always described someone who did more listening than talking, who didn't offer advice, someone who was truly and fully present, offering "a hand to hold, an understanding... hug."

APPLYING THE LESSON TO YOUR OWN LIFE

What career plans did you have when you were your students' age? Did you discern and follow your true vocation (i.e. the occupation to which God called you)? If so, what helped you hear and follow that call? If not, what kept you from hearing or following that call?

Spend a few minutes considering how your hand works, moves, feels. Can you understand Brand's fascination with the human hand?

In your lifetime, have you seen a trend toward specialization, or a trend toward generalization... in the medical field... in retail... in education... in the news media... in other industries? Which do you think is better, generalization or specialization? Why?

Does your congregation find and meet unmet needs in the community, or just duplicate what other churches and organizations are already doing? If the former, how did your congregation find its niche? If the latter, what would it take for your church to change and seek out its niche?

TEACHING THE LESSON
BY WHITNEY BROWN AND ANDY McCLUNG

SCRIPTURE
PSALM 39:13-16, EPHESIANS 2:22

LEADER PREP

RESOURCE LIST
- Song: "Better is One Day" by Matt Redman
- Media player for song
- Optional: Video player/Laptop Projector
- Copies of Ephesians text
- Optional: Videos ("Day of Discovery: The Story of Paul and Margaret Brand." https://vimeo.com/17777658) (https://youtu.be/wVVx_mU6Jq0)
- Pens/pencils
- Colored pencils
- Paper

BEFORE THE LESSON
Find the song "Better is One Day" by Matt Redman, and bring a media player to play the song. If you choose to show either of the videos, find and review the videos, and have them ready to play. Ask a church elder to join your group for the day to experience the lesson with the group and help with the closing activity.

GET STARTED

CALL TO WORSHIP (10-12min)
Have the song "Better is One Day," by Matt Redman playing as students enter.

Have someone read Psalm 84:1-2.

*How lovely is your dwelling place,
  O Lord of hosts!
My soul longs, indeed it faints
  for the courts of the Lord;
            my heart and my flesh sing for joy
  to the living God.*

CALL TO WAKE UP
Word Association:
Ask your students to share the first word or thought that comes to mind at the mention of each of the following words. Allow a moment for all to share their response before moving to the next word.

- **GIFT**
- **PAIN**
- **LEPROSY**
- **TEMPLE**
- **PEACE**
- **CALLING**

Option: Show this video clip about Paul & Margaret Brand to your students, "Day of Discovery: The Story of Paul and Margaret Brand." https://vimeo.com/17777658

LISTEN UP (20-25 min)
Read the Ephesians 2:13-22 passage aloud.

13 But now in Christ Jesus you who once were far off have been brought near by the blood of Christ. 14 For he is our peace; in his flesh he has made both groups into one and has broken down the dividing wall, that is, the hostility between us. 15 He has abolished the law with its commandments and ordinances, so that he might create in himself one new humanity in place of the two, thus making peace, 16 and might reconcile both groups to God in one body through the cross, thus putting to death that hostility through it. 17 So he came and proclaimed peace to you who were far off and peace to those who were near; 18 for through him both of us have access in one Spirit to the Father. 19 So then you are no longer strangers and aliens, but you are citizens with the saints and also members of the household of God, 20 built upon the foundation of the apostles and prophets, with Christ Jesus himself as the cornerstone. 21 In him the whole structure is joined together and grows into a holy temple in the Lord; 22 in whom you also are built together spiritually into a dwelling-place for God.

Activity: Have students read through the text again on their own using the printed copy. Using the colored pencils, tell them to highlight peaceful words/phrases in one color and non-peaceful words/phrases in a different color.

DISCUSSION QUESTIONS
When you close your eyes and envision peace, what do you see?

What does this passage teach you about the connections between Jesus, peace, pain, and you?

What stands out most to you in this passage?

What questions does this passage bring to your mind?

NOW WHAT? (10-15 min)
Journal Prompt: When Paul Brand was your age, he and his family had spent most of his life in India doing mission work. He was living in England when he quit school at 16 to learn construction, believing it would help him in the mission work he felt led to continue. He taught Sunday school and started a youth retreat center. Write a journal entry as Paul. What are you thinking/feeling as you try to figure out your place in the world?

Show the video from WBAL, Baltimore News, of Baltimore's clergy becoming agents of peace amidst violence between police and protestors as a current example of the church responding to the immediate needs of the community. (https://youtu.be/wVVx_mU6Jq0)

LIVE IT

LIVE IT (5-10 min)
Say: We are each given gifts. All of us know people in need in our broken and hurting world. We are called, together as the Body of Christ, to use our unique gifts to be "dwelling places for God by the Spirit." The gifts God gives us meet the great needs within our world, and that intersection of problems and solutions is where we find our call—both as individuals and as the church.

Paul Brand found his gifts in medicine and research, and in time found his call helping those who suffered from leprosy and those who suffered from ignorance about the disease.

Placing ourselves among those who are suffering helps us understand what Paul Brand describes as the "gift of pain." The struggles of others become our struggles, their pain becomes our pain, and in feeling the pain, we know something is wrong and we need to be made well. We rely on Christ to do the work and use the gifts God gives us to be agents of the peace of the Holy Spirit.

Activity 1: Give students colored pencils and a blank piece of paper, and give them the following instructions for making a Mind Map.

Mind Map
Using various colored pencils, write words and/or draw symbols around the blank paper that describe your passions and gifts. Then do the same thing, on the same paper, with the needs in your family, community, and the world you feel most compelled to help. (When completed, each student's gifts will be illustrated all over the paper alongside the needs they want to meet.)

Once students are finished, invite them to share and together see where you can find intersections between each person's gifts and the needs they could help heal.

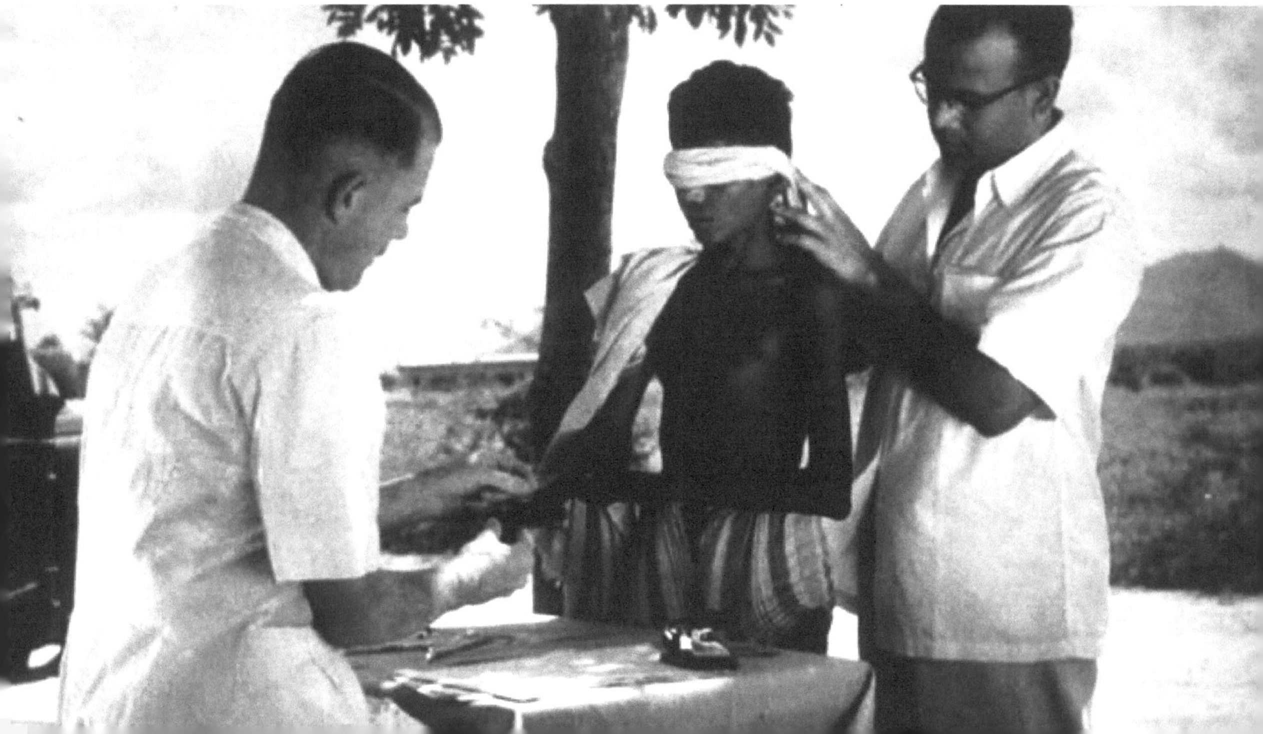

Activity 2: What is special about your church? What resources do you have (empty space, large congregation, craft supplies, a kitchen, showers, people with special skills, etc.)? What needs do you see in your community? How can the resources of your church be used to address those needs? Develop a plan, and decide what your role as a group will be in taking responsibility for that plan. Invite an elder to help you as you develop this plan, and present it to your church session to move your church into action in serving the needs of your community.

JUST IN CASE
If a student says something about how great it'd be not to feel pain, share the following. For those who can't feel pain, a bit of dust in the eye doesn't irritate the eye, so it never gets washed out and eventually leads to losing that eye. A splinter can lead to infection and the loss of a hand. Tying your shoes too tightly or loosely can cause a blister, which becomes infected, which becomes gangrenous, which leads to amputation. An internal injury or problem would go untreated until it caused serious damage or death just because, without pain, the person wouldn't know anything was wrong. God designed us to feel pain so we would know when something is wrong.

After finishing Activity 1 or 2 close with prayer.

NOTES

Resources used in compiling background material: Fearfully and Wonderfully Made by Paul Brand and Philip Yancey, "Job Hopping Is the 'New Normal' for Millennials" by Jeanne Meister on forbes.com, Soul Survivor by Philip Yancey, Ten Fingers for God by Dorothy Clarke Wilson. Photos used: "Dr. Paul Brand examines hands of a young leprosy patient" by Unknown photographer - http://goo.gl/UXG5vK, Paul Brand working on patient by Unknown photographer - http://goo.gl/jbXToC.

FAITH OUT LOUD

SOJOURNER TRUTH
BY JAMIE ADAMS AND ANDY McCLUNG

SCRIPTURE
JOEL 2:28-29, GALATIANS 3:28

THEME
Each person has a unique set of skills, gifts, experiences, and resources to be used in service to God.

LEADER INSIGHT

CONNECTING TO YOUR STUDENTS
Your students have probably heard this message before: "You're special just because you're you." Parents, educators, coaches, and churches have promoted this message for decades. While that message is well-intended and partially true, critics say it instills the mindset of "I'm already special, so why try harder or improve myself?" Some seasoned educators testify that former generations saw a low grade as incentive to work harder, but contemporary students see it as a personal insult; they feel they deserve a good grade just because they tried hard.

Perhaps the problem is the confusion between two different definitions of "special." Dictionary.com lists several definitions. The definition "having a specific or particular function, purpose, etc." is indeed true for each individual, created and gifted by God. The definition "different from what is ordinary or usual," however, does not apply to everyone. How could it?

The good news is that, in the Christian sense, the first definition is the most important.

EXPLAINING THE TOPIC
The woman known as Sojourner Truth was born a slave in New York, probably around 1797. (Dates of birth usually weren't recorded for slaves.) Her original owner named her Isabella. After thirty years of slavery to various owners, and giving birth to several children who became slaves, Isabella gained her freedom in 1827 (the year before New York outlawed slavery). Some sources say her final owner freed her; others say she escaped.

When she discovered that her five-year-old son had been illegally sold to a slave owner in Alabama, Isabella took the matter to court and won. This was the first time in the U.S. that an African-American woman won a court case against a Caucasian man.

Isabella moved to New York City in 1829. She eventually became a housekeeper for a Christian businessman, Elijah Pierson, who worked tirelessly to improve the plight of the city's poor, women, prostitutes, and minorities. Isabella was drawn to him because she, too, was a Christian interested in helping the powerless. Pierson had very progressive ideas for the time and did much ministry. Unfortunately, he went a little nuts after his wife died from tuberculosis. That's when he and Isabella became involved in a cult, which resulted in Pierson's murder and Isabella being falsely accused of that murder. Isabella filed a suit against her accusers, charging them with slander, and won.

Isabella says she had always, for her whole life, talked to God. But one day, while she was still a slave, she had a vision in which God revealed to her that God is everywhere. She said God gave her an "awful look," and she became overwhelmed with guilt over all the times she had not relied on God, and for all the promises she had made but not kept. She was certain that with another such look, her existence would be blown out like a candle. She began to wish for someone to stand between her and God, someone who wasn't unworthy like she was, someone who would plead with God on her behalf.

In her vision, someone did just that. She asked the figure, "Who are you?" The figure did not answer, but Isabella felt as if she both knew this person and didn't know him, all at the same time. Finally, she heard, "It is Jesus." She answered, "Yes, it is Jesus."

She had heard about Jesus before but had always understood him to be nothing more than a great man. This vision set her on a journey to learn more about Jesus. That journey included coming to understand that Jesus and God are one. She also came to understand that if Jesus could overcome the barrier between her—a sinful human—and all-powerful God, then Jesus could also overcome the barriers between persons with no power in society and those with all the power.

Led by God, Isabella changed her name to Sojourner Truth in 1843 and worked with others for the abolition of slavery. In 1850 a friend wrote and published her biography. Like most slaves, she was illiterate, so she dictated her life story to this friend. The book was a success. It made enough money that she could have settled down and lived out her days in peace. Instead, she used that money, and the book's success, to become a popular touring speaker. She travelled across the northern part of the U.S., speaking against slavery and championing women's rights.

Now, others were working with her.

Sojourner Truth spent the rest of her life in gratitude for what Jesus did for her, while working to end slavery and gain voting rights for women. Her work led her to meet President Abraham Lincoln in 1864, almost two years after he issued the Emancipation Proclamation and six months before the end of the Civil War. She told him that she'd never heard of him before he ran for president. He told her that he'd heard of her "many times before that." Sojourner only stopped touring and speaking when her health failed. She died on November 26, 1883.

What made this simple woman such a powerful force was a combination of her particular set of personality traits and personal experiences. She was strong, a hard worker, not a quitter, and not afraid to be the first to do something new. She could speak first-hand about the horrors of being owned by another person and of being treated as less than human. She learned from her experiences, both good and bad, and used her relationships with the right people to help her fulfill her mission. Above all, though, she took to heart what God showed her in that vision.

THEOLOGICAL UNDERPINNINGS
We find plenty of God-given, supernatural visions in the Bible. Today, however, someone who claims to have received a vision from God—not meaning an idea, goal, or specific calling, but a real supernatural vision—is often viewed as a nut. There are likely three reasons for this: 1) because so many nuts have falsely claimed to be following a vision from God when they did stupid, self-serving, and harmful things; 2) the messages from visions can be convicting and challenge people to change their comfortable lives; and, 3) ever since the coming of the Holy Spirit at Pentecost (in Acts 2), God has far more often revealed his will through the community rather than particular individuals. This is why visions are far more plentiful in the Old Testament than in the New.

While Sojourner could have been a successful abolitionist without being a Christian, she probably wouldn't have bothered. It was after becoming a Christian that she understood she couldn't stand by while others were powerless and oppressed. Additionally, by showing Sojourner that God was with her and could break through any human-made barrier, her vision inspired her to break through social barriers like gender, poverty, race, and her illiteracy.

Today some Christians seem to believe that being a Christian is only about a personal relationship with Jesus. To truly follow Christ, though, one must actively work to help the downcast, outcast, oppressed, and powerless. It's what Jesus did; it's what Sojourner did. It's what every Christian is called to do.

APPLYING THE LESSON TO YOUR OWN LIFE

What do you think of the "everybody is special" attitude? In the long run, does it do more good or more harm to individuals and society?

If you were to change your name based on your most significant spiritual experience, what would you change it to? Why?

How would you react to someone's claim to have had "a vision from God"? Why?

What group of people today is treated most similarly to how slaves were treated during Sojourner Truth's life? What group is most powerless in society today, like women were back then? Is this how God wants things to be?

Take a few minutes and list several of your personality traits. Then list several of your personal experiences. Then list the significant connections you have. Spend some time in prayerful consideration of these lists, trying to see how God might want to use your unique combination of traits and experiences.

SOJOURNER TRUTH
BY JAMIE ADAMS AND ANDY McCLUNG

SCRIPTURE
JOEL 2:28-29, GALATIANS 3:28

LEADER PREP

RESOURCE LIST
- Bibles
- Newsprint hung about the room
- Square sticky notes
- Digital camera/cell phone camera and dry erase markers
- Markers, pens, pencils
- Tape
- Digging Deeper quotes
- (Optional) Dry erase whiteboard
- (Optional) "Ain't I a Woman" speech https://www.youtube.com/watch?v=XilHJc9IZvE

BEFORE THE LESSON
You might want to read and/or watch a reenactment of Sojourner Truth's 1851 speech, "Ain't I a Woman." Depending on the maturity of your students, you may even want to share the video with your group. A word of caution though, the speech includes harsh language that would be considered highly taboo today.

Enlarge and print (or rewrite) the quotes on newsprint from the Digging Deeper section, and hang them on the wall throughout the room. Leave room on each piece of newsprint for students' thoughts to be added later.

GET STARTED

GET STARTED (10 minutes)
Give each student some square sticky notes and a marker or pencil. Have students write something that comes to mind when they read the quotes you've hung around the room (find the quotes in the Digging Deeper section). When students finish, they should stick their notes to the corresponding newsprint quote hanging in the room. Remind students that they do not have to identify themselves on the notes if they don't want to.

Once students are finished, have them share their thoughts on the activity if they want, but this isn't a necessary step. The quotes will be revisited at the end of the lesson, and some students may have different reactions to some of the quotes.

LISTEN UP

LISTEN UP (20 minutes)
Ask students if they have ever heard of Sojourner Truth. If they have, encourage them to share what they know. Depending on their responses, fill the gaps with background information above. If none of your students have any idea who she was, let them know that that isn't really surprising since she was both a woman and a slave, and for many people of the time, being just one of those would value the person insignificant and not worth time or attention.

After reviewing Truth's account of encountering God, ask students if they have ever known anyone who claimed to have seen God. Recount for them the explanations on Godly encounters in the Theological Underpinnings section. When considering how God interacts with people today, you might share a short personal testimony of a time you encountered God. From there, students may be compelled to share instances from their own lives.

Finally, spend some time on the racism and sexism that Truth experienced in her life. You might share the video "Ain't I a Woman" speech (https://www.youtube.com/watch?v=XilHJc9IZvE) at this time, or simply describe some of the extremely unjust treatment she underwent.

NOW WHAT

NOW WHAT? (15 minutes)
Allow time for discussion for each question.

Ask: Have you ever experienced or witnessed racism or sexism [you might need to define this term for the students]? How did you handle that?

Ask: In what forms do you see racism/sexism at school? In the community? In the news? What about at church?

DISCUSSION QUESTIONS

Ask: Is racism/sexism only about actions? Can people be racist/sexist with their words? What about with their silence?

Read Galatians 3:28
There is neither Jew nor Greek, there is neither slave nor free, there is no male and female, for you are all one in Christ Jesus.

Say: Considering this verse, how should we feel about racism and sexism, and all the other –ism(s) that exist?
Allow time for discussion.

Say: Do you think God loves all people equally? How could you know? Should we?
Allow time for discussion.

Say: Are we loving all people equally if we participate in these -isms? What about if we ignore the –isms?
Allow time for discussion

LIVE IT (5 minutes)
Ask students to consider the quotes and their responses they wrote. Give them the opportunity to change or add to their reactions. Review them briefly with the group.

Optional Activity
If time allows, have students, one at a time, sit with their head against the dry erase whiteboard. Have other students take turns drawing pictures or writing small phrases around the head of the person sitting. The pictures and phrases should be things that are special (really special) about the person and that make them valuable and unique to the youth group. Snap a picture of each student sitting in front of the board with his/her descriptions. Erase the board before they see it. Bring the developed/digital copies of the pictures to the students at their next meeting. (Pictures and a description of this activity can be found at https://goo.gl/RPJJCs.)

Remind students that our differences are to be celebrated, not judged. How boring would it be if everyone was exactly the same? Encourage them to be proud of the things that make them unique and to be encouragers to others who are different.

Close with this or a similar prayer: Dear God, thank you for creating people who are as different as day is from night. Help us to celebrate those differences in ourselves and others so we can stand up against all the –isms that plague our society.

DIGGING DEEPER
Here are some quotes from Sojourner Truth:
"Truth is powerful, and it prevails."

"Religion without humanity is poor human stuff."

"How came Jesus into the world? Through God who created him and woman who bore him. Man, where is your part?"

"I went to the Lord and asked Him to give me a new name. And the Lord gave me Sojourner, because I was to travel up and down the land, showing the people their sins, and being a sign unto them."

"Does not God love colored children as well as white children? And did not the same Savior die to save the one as well as the other? If so, white children must know that if they go to Heaven, they must go there without their prejudice against color, for in Heaven black and white are one in the love of Jesus. Now children, remember what Sojourner Truth has told you, and thus get rid of your prejudice... that you may be all the children of your Father who is in Heaven."

NOTES

Resources used in compiling background material: Biography.com, Conversions by Hugh Kerr and John Mulder, oxfordscholarship.com, sojournertruth.org Photos used: CDV of Sojourner Truth owned by Wright's New York Gallery / Battlecreek, Mich. https://goo.gl/43H6Sj, Tunnel Vision by Alexander Mueller with contrast additions - https://goo.gl/6MOfkF, Modeling @ Christmas by Prayitno with cut out edits and words added - https://goo.gl/A3N47d

FAITH OUT LOUD

BROTHER ANDREW
BY JAMIE ADAMS AND ANDY McCLUNG

SCRIPTURE
MATTHEW 5:10-11, LUKE 10:1-4, 1 CORINTHIANS 12:26-27, MATTHEW 5:43-44

THEME
Living as a Christian does not mean a tame, safe, boring life.

LEADER INSIGHT

CONNECTING TO YOUR STUDENTS
Many teens say church is boring, and it's hard to disagree. What do we do at church, whether it's worship, Sunday school, or youth group? We sit still. We sit still and listen to a sermon or lesson. We sit still and pray. We sit still and read. This perception of church as boring is worse than it seems at first because in teens' minds, the idea (or fact) that church is boring translates into Christianity being boring. But, if done right, church will reinforce that Christianity is anything but boring.

Most churches focus on ministry to teens, which is where much of the sitting comes in. A focus on ministry done by teens is equally important. Mission projects are a great way to put some movement and action into teens' spiritual lives—building something, putting together care packages, making something. Mission trips are even better. During this lesson, refer to some mission projects or trips you've heard teens talk about.

EXPLAINING THE TOPIC
Andrew van der Bijl was born in Holland in 1928. His family of eight lived in the smallest house in the small, poor town of Witte. Andrew's family went to church, but he found it boring and usually sneaked out. When his handicapped brother died from tuberculosis, 11 year old Andrew gave up on God.

> Andrew became known as Brother Andrew not because he's clergy,
> but because he's a "brother" to all Christians.

In 1940, the Nazis took over Holland. Andrew says he had always "dreamed of derring-do," playing spies and war as a child. When the Nazis stationed a few soldiers in unimportant Witte, they shut down the school, turned off the electricity, and raided all the gardens. Andrew secretly sabotaged their car and threw fireworks at them. Holland was freed in 1945.

When, at 17, Andrew joined the army and left home for some real-life derring-do, his mother gave him a Bible. Andrew, knowing he wouldn't, promised to read it. He became a commando to fight the communists who had taken over some Dutch colonies. He loved the adventure of training but was disgusted with actual combat. After a mission in which he helped massacre an entire village of non-combatants, Andrew went "nearly mad" for two years. He lived as if he was suicidal, earning accolades as a fierce commando. Then a bullet in the ankle took him out of combat.

Andrew's buddies put that Bible beside his hospital bed. He left it there. Then one day, he asked one of the Franciscan nuns who served as orderlies why they were so cheerful in that horrid place. She tapped his Bible and said, "It's the love of Christ. You've got the answer right here." Twenty-year-old Andrew started reading that Bible. Then, with help of a pen pal half a world away, he started studying it. Just before he left the hospital, one of the nuns asked what he was holding on to that was keeping him from being free.
When Andrew was sent home, partially crippled, he ignored God for several months, even attending a revival while drunk just to heckle. But something led him back to the Bible, then back to church, and then to realize that holding on to his ego was keeping him from being free. He prayed, "Lord, if you show me the way, I will follow you." God did show him the way. At another revival, this one attended in earnest, Andrew answered the call to mission work.

He worried that his bad ankle would keep him from doing good work in the mission field, but when he finally put his worries aside completely and promised to trust God fully, his ankle was miraculously healed. Andrew overcame many obstacles to undergo two years of missionary training. The missionary school focused on trusting God to provide, and time after time Andrew saw that when he or others stepped out in faith to do good, God provided what was needed.

In 1955, with his preparation finished at age 27, Andrew went to Poland and discovered a small Christian community, active but persecuted under communism. On a trip to Czechoslovakia he saw more of the subtle, but crushing, persecution of Christians under communism; public Christians wouldn't be hired or accepted into schools, and Bibles were very scarce. That's when Andrew found his niche—smuggling Bibles into communist countries. He had no money, no support network, and no plan. But he knew those issues would be no problem for God. Back home he wrote a magazine article about his experience, and people started sending money to help; someone even gave him a Volkswagen Beetle!

On his next trip into Yugoslavia in 1957, he hid a few Bibles in the Beetle. When he got to the border he saw the guards were inspecting each car, and he knew the Bibles would be found easily. So he prayed and relied on God. His car and luggage were inspected, but the Bibles somehow weren't noticed. Similar encounters happened time after time, with soldiers sometimes spending an hour inspecting other cars but just waving Andrew through. Eventually he stopped hiding the Bibles at all so he could carry more. He knew he was risking imprisonment for himself and those to whom he was smuggling Bibles, but he'd always wanted an exciting life. And this excitement wasn't just for fun, but truly for a good cause.

A network of people grew to help Andrew in his work, which spread to China. Christians in communist countries amazed him with their ability to maintain hope and faith in Christ under persecution. His mere presence reminded them that the Church is bigger than any one congregation, denomination, or nation. European communism fell in 1989, but Andrew kept working, switching his focus to Muslim-controlled countries in which Christians were persecuted.

THEOLOGICAL UNDERPINNINGS

Andrew sees parallels between the spread of communism 60 years ago and the spread of fundamental Islam today, and he regrets that some people on the outside assume that all Muslims are terrorists. He found that the mission of Christians being oppressed in Islamic-controlled countries should be the same as those in communist-controlled countries: when Christians focus on being for Christ, rather than against something else, priorities are in order and everything else falls into place.

Andrew learned early that successful mission work starts with presence; you can't minister to someone effectively unless you're there with them. Presence first, service second. It's much easier for someone to hear you say Jesus loves them if you've already made them feel loved by being with them and meeting their needs. Andrew says, "First, earn the right to get their attention; then show them Jesus—perhaps not with words but always with actions." Loving communists and Muslims isn't easy, he says, especially when they're persecuting our fellow believers. But it's what Jesus told us to do in Matthew 5:43-44.

Andrew's story is full of situations when he relied on God to provide what was needed: a train ticket, money for Bibles, an interpreter, a distracted customs agent, meeting just the right person with just the right connections, etc. Our Confession of Faith testifies to God's providential care as well, assuring us that God does indeed act in our lives to provide what we need to carry out the mission of the Church, and that while sometimes we can see and understand why God provides what and when God does, other times it remains a mystery (see 1.13-1.18).

APPLYING THE LESSON TO YOUR OWN LIFE
How many Bibles could you gather in a few hours? Imagine having to answer that with, "None." Do a YouTube search for "getting Bibles for the first time."

When have you had to completely rely on God for something? What was it like, having no control over what happened?

Andrew learned that in some communist countries, the government had more influence over children—through heavy propaganda, control of the schools, and the news—than their parents did. Could that happen in the U.S.? If so, what would it take for that to happen? If not, what would keep it from happening?

How often do you think of your class, your congregation, your denomination as just a tiny part of the worldwide Church? How often is this emphasized in your congregation? How does your congregation support missions?

Taking Matthew 5:44 seriously, Andrew says that for him, Islam means, "I sincerely love all Muslims." How seriously do you take this verse?

BROTHER ANDREW
BY JAMIE ADAMS AND ANDY McCLUNG

SCRIPTURE
MATTHEW 5:10-11, LUKE 10:1-4, 1 CORINTHIANS 12:26-27, MATTHEW 5:43-44

LEADER PREP

RESOURCE LIST
- Bibles
- Paper and pencils
- Information about mission opportunities for your students
- YouTube videos :
    - Indonesian Tribe received Bible for the First Time
      https://www.youtube.com/watch?v=bZFPtpZcs0Q
    - Chinese Christians See Bible for the First Time
      https://www.youtube.com/watch?v=nznUNowHYH0
    - Brother Andrew – « God's Smuggler »
      https://www.youtube.com/watch?v=srncqLLIZ2I

BEFORE THE LESSON
Research some local service work opportunities in your area. Some suggestions are Habitat for Humanity, Salvation Army, and other food banks or thrift stores. If there are none in your area, consider working with other churches in your area to plan a community clean up day.

If you have anyone in your church who has been on a mission trip to a place where Bibles and churches are not as commonplace as in the U.S., invite them to come share their experiences with your students.

GET STARTED

GET STARTED (10 minutes)
If you have someone who has been on a mission trip to another country where Christianity is uncommon, introduce them and let them share with your students some stories and/or pictures from their trip. Allow and encourage time for questions and answers.

If you don't have someone who can give first hand experience, show one of the YouTube videos of people receiving Bibles for the first time.

Ask: Would you be that excited if someone gave you a Bible? Why or why not?

Say: Do you get that excited about church? Why or why not?

Pass out the paper and pencils. Have students take two pieces of paper each. Instruct them to write their favorite thing about youth group/church on one and their least favorite thing on another. Instruct them to wad up their "likes" paper, and throw them to the left side of the room. Then, have them wad up their "dislikes," and throw them to the right side of the room. Leave the papers on the floor until the end of the lesson.

LISTEN UP (20 minutes)
Review the life and experiences of Brother Andrew from the Explaining the Topic section. Make sure you paint a vivid picture of what it would have been like, smuggling Bibles into a place. For most of your students, they won't be able to imagine a world where that would be a dangerous endeavor. For some of your students, stories of spying and smuggling will be intriguing.

Highlight that Brother Andrew found himself in places where he often could do nothing but rely on God. (You might want to show a section of this YouTube video to illustrate this: https://www.youtube.com/watch?v=srncqLLIZ2I)

Allow time for discussion after each question.

Ask: When you think about doing work for God, what does that involve?

Say: Before this story, did you ever consider that working for God could involve spying and smuggling? Why?

Ask: Have you ever had to completely rely on someone else for something, maybe even something that could put you in danger? How did that make you feel?

Say: Do you think you could ever completely rely on God like that? Why or why not?

Close the discussion focusing on Brother Andrew's lesson of "presence first, service second."

Ask: What do you think Andrew meant by that philosophy?

Remind them that in Brother Andrew's ministry, he wasn't just dropping off Bibles and going back home. He took the time to get to know the people. It would have been much quicker to assume they were all uninterested in Christianity because of the leadership of the country, but Brother Andrew spent time with the people, realized they didn't fit the stereotype of people in those regions, and he began to truly get to know them. It was from that point on that the true Gospel message began to be spread.

NOW WHAT? (15 minutes)
Challenge your students to make changes in their own ways of viewing the people around them. Tell them that, like Brother Andrew, they are part of the body of the Church, and as such, are just as capable of enacting positive change around them in the name of God.

Review the likes and dislikes written on the tossed paper from the church likes/dislikes activity in the Get Started section. Make a list of what the students have shared. There's no reason to point out who said what. From that list, encourage

the students to brainstorm ways they can make what they like already even better. For things they don't like, develop a plan of action the students can implement to address it. (This might be a golden opportunity to involve the youth in some of the inner workings of your church. Invite them to sit in on session or planning meetings to present their ideas.)

Help the students come up with something small they can do within the next few weeks. A successful change, no matter how small, will impact your students greatly by showing them that they are, indeed, a valuable instrument of the church.

LIVE IT (5 minutes)
If you have local opportunities, establish a work day where the students can get some hands-on experience working with people. Even if there aren't places where they can build houses or feed homeless nearby, they could still visit a nursing home during a game hour or give away popsicles on a hot day at the park. The idea is to get your students in places where they can get to know people they would otherwise never stop to talk to.

Finally, close with this or a similar prayer: Awesome God, thank you for your providence in our lives. Even when we don't realize it, you put people in our paths and opportunities for us to be missionaries. Open our eyes to those opportunities. Help us to be present in people's lives, just as you are ever present in ours. Amen.

JUST IN CASE
If a student asks what persecution against Christians looks like today, share these statistics from opendoors.org. Each month 322 Christians are killed for their faith, 772 acts of violence (beatings, abductions, rape, arrest, forced marriages) are committed against Christians, and 214 churches and Christian-owned properties are destroyed.

NOTES

Resources used in compiling background material: God's Smuggler by Brother Andrew, et al, inspirationalchristians.org, opendoors.org. Photos used: Brother Andrew Biography Photo used from Inspirational Christians - http://goo.gl/8fmMjK, Blue Beetle by Andrey with poster edges and cut out effect additions - https://goo.gl/tSc4h5, Stack of Bibles by Bright Adventures with poster edges and cut out effect additions - https://goo.gl/CrKz1j

FAITH OUT LOUD

CORRIE TEN BOOM
BY WHITNEY BROWN AND ANDY McCLUNG

SCRIPTURE
JAMES 2:14-26, GENESIS 22:1-14, JOSHUA 2:1-24

THEME
When they're born from true compassion, our prayers for others lead to action.

LEADER INSIGHT

CONNECTING TO YOUR STUDENTS
Any honest assessment of American Christianity must conclude that we've had it pretty easy. It's probably hard for your students to grasp the idea of being physically beaten for possessing a Bible, or risking one's life to attend worship.

This lesson will showcase a completely foreign world.

Even if your students have studied the Holocaust in school or learned of it from a book or movie, its horror and terror is still difficult to grasp. A quick web search for holocaust images would be disturbingly enlightening. Like Mr. Rogers said, though: when seeing images of scary things, look for the people helping. Corrie ten Boom and her family were those helpers in the midst of perhaps the most atrocious act in history.

Your students may engage in intercessory prayers regularly. They may do regular mission work. But do they recognize the connection between the two actions?

EXPLAINING THE TOPIC
Corrie ten Boom was born in Holland in 1892, the fourth child in a Christian family. The family ran a watch shop out of their home, but had little money. From her parents, Corrie learned that prayer and hospitality are parts of being a Christian, and that the Jewish people are special to God. She accepted Christ at the age of five, and thereafter was known for her compassion and intercessory prayers, both of which usually focused on people the world saw as unimportant—the drunks stumbling home from bars on her street, those with mental developmental issues, her poor or Jewish neighbors. Corrie was also an early proponent for women, beginning girls' clubs for teens to have a place for recreation and spiritual growth.

In the 1930s after the Nazi party took over their own government in Germany, they began to invade neighboring countries. In 1940 they took over Holland. Corrie was in her 40s and running the family watch shop. German soldiers soon were everywhere. Then food was rationed and curfews imposed. Then the persecution of the Jewish residents began. "Jews Forbidden" signs went up; Jewish-owned shops were closed; and all Jews were forced to wear the star of David. Then the Nazis started gathering up Jewish people and sending them away from their homes. No one knew, at first, that they were being sent to concentration camps to be murdered. No one could imagine that six million Jews would be murdered before the war was over.

Corrie's family took in Jewish friends, neighbors, and strangers to hide them from the Nazis. This turned into an organized local underground resistance movement, hiding dozens of refugees in various homes and sneaking them out of the country when possible. Corrie and her underground workers also helped German soldiers who deserted after realizing Hitler was evil.

Corrie worked out a complex system with the underground. A certain sign in the shop window would mean it was safe to enter, and information was exchanged in coded conversations right in front of Germans. Eventually, Corrie began coordinating with the broader underground resistance movement. They were the ones who sent men to smuggle in tools and materials to build a secret room in Corrie's house. When Nazi search parties came in the shop, someone would sound a hidden buzzer. The refugees would quickly enter the hiding place through a sliding panel under the bottom shelf of a bookshelf. Seven people often hid in this room, which was only thirty inches deep.

In February of 1944, it all fell apart. The Nazis knew Corrie was harboring Jews. They knew about the underground network. The shop and house were raided, but the hiding place wasn't found. Corrie and her sister, both in their 50s, were beaten, arrested, and sent to prison. Their father, 92, was arrested too. He died ten days later. Other family members were arrested and released. Guards were stationed at the house, but the people in the hiding place escaped.

Imprisoned in her own country, Corrie still treated others with kindness, other inmates and guards alike. One lieutenant, after Corrie talked to him about Jesus, destroyed files taken from Corrie's house that would have gotten many more people arrested and executed. This same man tried, unsuccessfully, to get Corrie and her sister released.

As the Allies advanced into Holland, Corrie and her sister were moved to concentration camps in Germany. Corrie managed to smuggle in a Bible. She used it to bring herself and others encouragement and comfort in that horrible place. She often broke camp rules, risking beatings or death, to help others.

Late in 1944, Corrie's sister told her that after the war God wanted them to open a healing center for concentration camp survivors. She died the next day from illness. Then, inexplicably, Corrie was released. Someone made a clerical error. Corrie took a difficult journey home, finding Holland war-ravaged but partially liberated. Knowing she was being watched, she couldn't work with the underground anymore. They raised some money for her, though. She reopened the watch shop and opened the doors of her home to the mentally handicapped.

> Corrie only learned of the clerical error in 1959 on a return to the camp to honor the 96,000 women killed at this camp. She was supposed to be gassed the week after her release.

When the war was over, Corrie started the healing center. Her criterion for knowing when someone was healed was that they could forgive. She also toured the country, speaking about the horrors of the concentration camps and the mercy of Jesus. Her popularity as a speaker took her throughout Europe and the U.S. People would often approach her or write her to say that during the war she had spoken words of encouragement to them, prayed with them, helped their loved ones, or that they had simply observed her compassion and faith, and had been moved to accept Jesus for themselves.

Corrie died in 1983, but only after her books about her experiences had become best sellers and a popular movie had been made from one of them. So even after her death, her encouragement to forgive and experience true compassion continues.

THEOLOGICAL UNDERPINNINGS
Pity is feeling sorry for someone in a bad situation. We can feel and express pity while remaining "above" the bad situation. Compassion is caring so much about someone in need that we can't help but to show them kindness. Compassion leads us to enter into the other person's misery with them. Corrie ten Boom practiced compassion, not pity.

Corrie also practiced an effective style of evangelism. She was bold and direct, but she didn't scream from a street corner, telling passersby they're going to hell unless they repent right now. Her actions of compassion and helping paved the way for people to hear her tell them the good news of salvation through Jesus. Her story is full of people whom she led to Christ who then led others to Christ. The secret of her evangelistic success may be that she did what she needed to in order to tell others about Jesus, but she didn't try to do the Holy Spirit's job. It is the Holy Spirit who convicts people of their sins and the need for repentance (see Confession of Faith 4.01-4.02). Also, she never seems to have tried to convert Jews into Christians, but respected that they are God's chosen people.

People in horrible situations—and it doesn't get any worse than living in a Nazi concentration camp—are more likely to turn to God than continue to rely on themselves or whatever they have been drawing on for spiritual support. Perhaps that is why so many middle-class American Christians' evangelistic efforts have been fruitless: they've been trying to evangelize people who are quite comfortable. Their efforts may produce more Christians (but not necessarily financially contributing church members) if aimed at the sick, the imprisoned, the addicted, the desperate. (Ironically, that Christianity lends itself to, and focuses on, the marginalized is one of the reasons some people criticize the faith.)

APPLYING THE LESSON TO YOUR OWN LIFE
Recall any stories from family members who witnessed the effects of the Holocaust, or any stories you know of it from your own reading and education. If you're unfamiliar with the Holocaust, spend a few minutes browsing ushmm.org, the website of the United States Holocaust Museum. Imagine what you would have done, had you been a Christian in a country the Nazis took over.

Have you ever been in danger of, or suffered, arrest or physical harm for doing what you believed was morally right? If not, for what beliefs would you take such risks? If so, were your actions born from a socio-political stance, or from a theological belief? Is there a difference?

Which do you pray more often: for God to "be with" people in need (sick, hungry, bereaved, homeless) or for God to use you to help people in need? Can we Christians be answers to our own prayers?

JUST IN CASE
If your students don't seem to recognize how they might help in a situation like the Holocaust, share this story: Before she was arrested, Corrie heard about a Nazi plan to raid a Jewish orphanage and kill all the babies. She told the teenagers of the underground to come up with a plan to save them. She didn't want to know details so, if captured, she couldn't give away the plan. The teenage boys, dressed in German uniforms taken from deserters whom the underground helped, pretended to conduct the raid and took the babies. The teenage girls helped every single baby find a new home. About one hundred babies were saved that day.

CORRIE TEN BOOM
BY WHITNEY BROWN AND ANDY McCLUNG

SCRIPTURE
JAMES 2:14-26, GENESIS 22:1-14, JOSHUA 2:1-24

LEADER PREP

RESOURCES
- Masking tape
- Video player for virtual tour
- Virtual tour of the Corrie ten Boom Museum (http://tenboom.com/en/)
- Handout of bookmarks
- Copy of your church's prayer list
- A small space (A square barely large enough for your group, taped on the floor would work. This is symbolic of the ten Boom's hiding place. See "Call to Wake Up.")

BEFORE THE LESSON
Review the link to the Unites States Holocaust Memorial Museum to prepare yourself for potential questions your students might ask about the Holocaust.

Tape an appropriately sized square/rectangle on the floor to create your "hiding place."

Review the virtual tour of the Corrie ten Boom Museum, especially sections 8-13, and have it prepared to play on your media player.

Make as many copies of the bookmarks in this lesson as needed for your students on thick paper, and cut them before your students arrive.

Find a copy of your church's prayer list, and make sure you know the needs of the people listed.

GET STARTED

CALL TO WAKE UP
Create a small space, barely large enough for all of your students to fit uncomfortably, and conduct the majority of the lesson from within this space. Use items in your classroom to outline the space, or just use tape to make an appropriately sized rectangle on the floor.

As students enter the room, quietly rush them into the space.

CALL TO WORSHIP
Have someone read this quote from Corrie ten Boom on prayer:

"We never know how God will answer our prayers, but we can expect that He will get us involved in His plan for the answers. If we are true intercessors, we must be ready to take part in God's work on behalf of the people for whom we pray."

LISTEN UP

LISTEN UP (20-25 minutes)
James 2:14-26

₁₄What good is it, my brothers and sisters, if you say you have faith but do not have works? Can faith save you? ₁₅If a brother or sister is naked and lacks daily food, ₁₆and one of you says to them, "Go in peace; keep warm and eat your fill," and yet you do not supply their bodily needs, what is the good of that? ₁₇So faith by itself, if it has no works, is dead.

₁₈But someone will say, "You have faith and I have works." Show me your faith without works, and I by my works will show you my faith. ₁₉You believe that God is one; you do well. Even the demons believe—and shudder. ₂₀Do you want to be shown, you senseless person, that faith without works is barren? ₂₁Was not our ancestor Abraham justified by works when he offered his son Isaac on the altar? ₂₂You see that faith was active along with his works, and faith was brought to completion by the works. ₂₃Thus the scripture was fulfilled that says, "Abraham believed God, and it was reckoned to him as righteousness," and he was called the friend of God. ₂₄You see that a person is justified by works and not by faith alone.

₂₅Likewise, was not Rahab the prostitute also justified by works when she welcomed the messengers and sent them out by another road? ₂₆For just as the body without the spirit is dead, so faith without works is also dead.

Activity: After reading the passage, divide your class into three groups. Assign each group one of the following readings, and ask them to come up with a summary together. The first two are the stories mentioned in the scripture above.

Group 1: Abraham – Genesis 22:1-14
Group 2: Rahab – Joshua 2:1-24
Group 3: Corrie ten Boom – allow this group to read from the "Explaining the Topic" section of this lesson plan to learn about Corrie's life.

After all three groups have finished reading and summarizing; ask them to share with the whole group.

DISCUSSION QUESTIONS

What stands out to you most in this passage from James?

How does Corrie ten Boom's life help you better understand James 2:14-26?

Can you think of a time when someone has showed you their faith by the way they treated you or someone else? What was that like?

DISCUSSION QUESTIONS

NOW WHAT? (10-15 minutes)

Activity 1: The Corrie ten Boom Museum has a virtual tour of the ten Boom house on their website (http://tenboom.com/en/). Take the tour with your students. The "hiding place" explanation begins on point number 8 in the tour. If you are limited on time, begin here and go through point 13. Point 13 is the actual "hiding place"; use the navigational arrows at the bottom of the screen to look at the full view of the small space.

Activity 2: Come out of your "hiding place." Invite students to share what that experience was like for them. How would their thoughts and attitudes about being in that small space have been different if their life and safety depended on staying there for hours?

While teaching this lesson, students may have questions about the Holocaust. The United States Holocaust Memorial Museum has resources available for teachers, including commonly asked questions: http://www.ushmm.org/educators/teaching-about-the-holocaust/common-questions

LIVE IT (5-10 minutes)

Look at your church's prayer list. Choose someone for whom you will intercede, either as individuals or as a group. How will you become involved in God's answer to that prayer?

Give each student a bookmark. Invite them to write the name of the person for whom they will pray and what they intend to do as a part of that prayer on the back of the bookmark. Tell them to take it with them to be reminded to be in prayer for that person.

Resources used in compiling background material: Corrie: the Lives She's Touched by Joan Winmill Brown, The Hiding Place by Corrie ten Boom, tenboom.org. Photos used: "Corrie-ten-Boom2" used from "A Christian Worldview of Fiction" - http://goo.gl/hKAanm, "Holocaust Memorial" by Milan Boers - https://goo.gl/qEmgnz, "Holocaust Memorial" by Milan Boers - https://goo.gl/8mVDb5, "Secret rooms in the library" by Marcin Wichary with coloration edits - https://goo.gl/7LYzo5

FAITH OUT LOUD

C. S. LEWIS
BY JAMIE ADAMS AND ANDY McCLUNG

SCRIPTURE
PROVERBS 13:20

THEME
Being a Christian doesn't mean not using your brain.

LEADER INSIGHT

CONNECTING TO YOUR STUDENTS
Some of your students probably know of Lewis' Narnia books, or saw the recent movie adaptations. If so, don't dwell on this familiarity. Lewis was far more than a children's author. (The Narnia books are far more than children's books, too, but that's how they've been marketed.) Your students may have heard the pastor quote Lewis from the pulpit, which may be a better connection to exploit. Many of those outside the Christian faith consider Christians gullible, unintelligent, superstitious, and either ignorant or ignoring of scientific fact. (Many Christians would happily agree they ignore science.) Your students may have encountered this derision on some level and been made to feel as if they have to choose between what Christianity says is true and what super-smart people say is true.

Knowing C. S. Lewis can dispel that myth. He was super-smart (knew Greek, Latin, Italian, German, French, and more) and a Christian.

EXPLAINING THE TOPIC
Clive Staples Lewis was born in Belfast, Ireland, in 1898. When he was about four years old, he decided he didn't like his name and told his family to call him "Jacksie." The nickname stuck and was later shortened to "Jack." The Lewis house was very large with lots of corridors and unused rooms to explore. Lewis says there also were "endless books." There were books in every room of the house and on the landing of the staircase, two deep in the bookcases, and stacked shoulder-high in the attic. Lewis was allowed to read whatever he wished, and he read a lot. He also wrote stories, creating a magical land and a complete history and detailed maps for it. He played outside a lot, too, but disfigured thumbs kept him from building things and playing sports.

Lewis was not interested in religion, but he loved mythology. When he was 9, his mother died from cancer. He says, "...all settled happiness, all that was tranquil and reliable, disappeared from my life." How his father handled the tragedy drove him and Lewis apart. That same year, 1908, Lewis went to his first boarding school. Lewis describes the schools as terrible places, his only joy coming from a few good teachers. When he was 13, Lewis became an atheist. He was very good at academics, debate, and logical thought. He began college at Oxford University, but World War I interrupted his education. He entered the army at 19 and saw action. He was wounded a year later and returned to finish college at Oxford, becoming a literature professor there. He became friends with several Christians, all intellectuals like him. Throughout his life, Lewis was to befriend or come under the tutelage (in person or through their writings) of many intelligent people. Conversing, discussing, challenging, and debating with them helped sharpen Lewis' own intellect. When he was 27, Lewis heard a devout atheist—"the cynic of cynics, the toughest of the toughs"—say that the evidence for the historical authenticity of the gospels was surprisingly good, and, "It almost looks as if it had really happened." Over the next three years, Lewis felt compelled to re-read many of his favorite books and now noticed God-affirming themes in them. The idea that God might be real terrified Lewis. He says, "You must picture me alone in that room…night after night, feeling…the steady, unrelenting approach of Him I so earnestly desired not to meet."

This man who had risen to the heights of intellectual reason came to understand that, as he put it, "God was Reason itself." Then, in 1929, at the age of 30, Lewis gave in to God. He knelt and, as "the most reluctant convert in all of England," prayed for the first time since he was a child.

But Lewis was not yet a Christian. He started attending church, but didn't think much of it, all the while continuing the conversations with his Christian friends. Then one night in 1931, when Lewis was 32, he had a long talk with two friends, Hugo Dyson and J. R. R. Tolkien, both Christians and professors. About a week later, while riding to the zoo in the sidecar of his brother's motorcycle, Lewis quietly became a Christian.

"When we set out I did not believe that Jesus Christ was the Son of God, and when we reached the zoo I did. Yet I had not exactly spent the journey in thought. Nor in great emotion." Lewis finally accepted the only reasonable answer to his question about Christianity.

Lewis, Dyson, Tolkien, and others gathered together weekly for many years, sharing their in-progress writings, critiquing and encouraging one another. Again, Lewis surrounded himself with people who would challenge him.

In 1954 Lewis began teaching Medieval and Renaissance Literature at Cambridge, a position created for him. At 57 Lewis secretly married Joy Gresham, a divorced New Yorker with two young boys, in a civil ceremony to give her British citizenship. They'd been friends for five years, her brashness causing a stir in Lewis' stuffy British academic circles. The next year they got married for real. Joy, formerly Jewish, then communist, then atheist, and finally Christian (due in part to Lewis' writings), was another person who challenged Lewis' thinking. Joy died from cancer four years later.

Lewis, suffering from several medical problems and only a few days shy of his 65th birthday, died on November 22, 1963, the same day as John F. Kennedy. A prolific and popular writer and teacher during his life, he has become even more so since his death. Most of the books he wrote have remained in print; dozens of books have been written about him; teachers and preachers constantly quote him in lessons and sermons; and just about everything he ever wrote has been published, including unfinished manuscripts, personal letters, poems, his diaries, his childhood stories, and academic papers.

C. S. Lewis was a great thinker and teacher. He continues to be a friend to those who like to be challenged to keep their thinking sharp.

THEOLOGICAL UNDERPINNINGS

Lewis was taught early on that it's not enough to say something is wrong; you have to prove it's wrong first. Adopting this practice made Lewis a great debater, for he had already mentally proved his opponent wrong before the debate began. It also helped defeat his atheism, as he could never prove God doesn't exist. When the Christian Lewis was confronted with the idea that the universe was born when the right particles happened to collide and that humans developed when the right chemicals happened to bump into each other, he responded by arguing that if the human mind was a random accident, then any thoughts from that mind would be accidental, and it makes no sense to trust accidental atom movements to give logical explanations of anything. That, he said, would be like looking at a puddle of spilled milk and expecting it to explain how the jug was made and why it was tipped over.

Lewis says that the works of Christian authors and the words of Christian friends brought him to the point where he could feel God closing in on him to make a decision. He says he knew he had the freedom to choose, but at the same time felt as if it "did not really seem possible" not to choose to believe. This fits with Cumberland Presbyterian theology. "The Holy Spirit works through... the witness of believers", moving "on the hearts of sinners, convincing them of... their need for salvation." This call "precedes all desire, purpose, and intention of the sinner to come to Christ," and "Persons may resist and reject this call" (Confession of Faith 4.02-4.04). Lewis was free to choose not to believe, but as a reasoning person, he had to believe because God makes sense.

Lewis was a theologian and an apologist. An apologist is one who practices apologetics (which has nothing to do with saying you're sorry). Apologetics is "the branch of theology concerned with the defense or proof of Christianity." It's interesting that such an influential theologian and effective apologist was also a layperson with no formal theological education.

APPLYING THE LESSON TO YOUR OWN LIFE

Have you ever felt as if you were expected to leave your brains at the door when entering church for worship or Bible study? Do educational opportunities in your congregation strive to encourage growth through challenges, or simply affirm what folks already think…or, even worse, just tell people what to think?

How do your friendships challenge you to grow spiritually, intellectually, in other ways? How does your marriage?

How do you respond to the following Lewis quote?
"*If you are thinking of becoming a Christian, I warn you, you are embarking on something which is going to take the whole of you, brains and all.*"

If you've never read Lewis, challenge yourself to read one of his books. If you have read Lewis, challenge yourself to read more of his works and tell others about him.

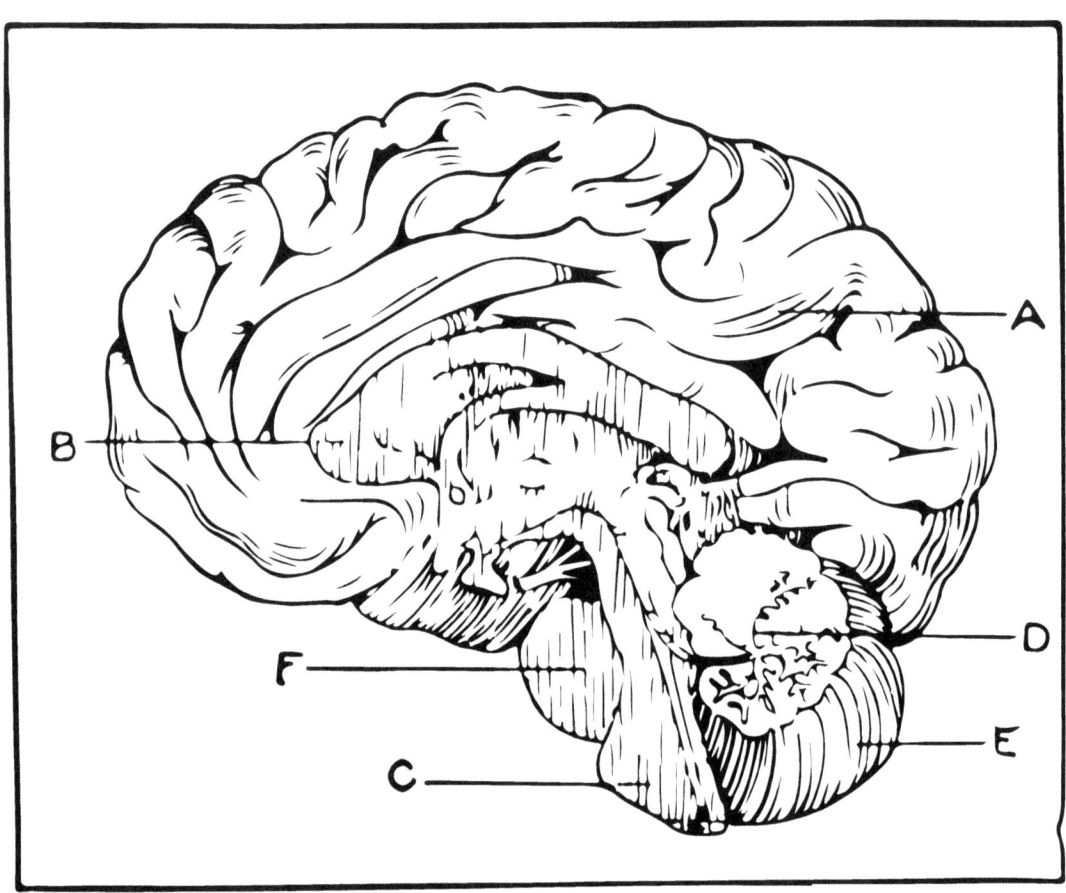

BRAIN

C. S. LEWIS
BY JAMIE ADAMS AND ANDY McCLUNG
SCRIPTURE
PROVERBS 13:20

LEADER PREP

RESOURCE LIST
- Bibles
- Small candies/prizes
- Blind fold
- Masking tape or rope (to mark a course)
- Copies of the "Digging Deeper" page for students
- Various "obstacles" such as throw pillows or small soft toys
- "Religion and Science by C.S. Lewis Doodle" YouTube video (https://www.youtube.com/watch?v=AJu0oYvi-cY)

LEADER PREP
Familiarize yourself with a few concepts your students may have encountered in their school studies that tend to cause religious controversy, like the Big Bang Theory.

GET STARTED

GET STARTED (10 minutes)
Begin the lesson with a quick Q&A session. Keep it fast, and reward answers with small candies and/or prizes of some sort. Begin with simple, easy questions, progressing to more difficult ones, leading eventually to some that do not have absolute answers. The idea is to lead students to the point where their faith and their education may not be easily reconciled. Encourage debate, but do not focus on "right" or "wrong" answers.

Feel free to use the questions below or create some of your own:

- What is the name of the planet on which we live? (Earth)
- What is a baby cow called? (calf)
- What do tadpoles become? (frogs)
- What grows from a planted acorn? (tree)
- How old is the Earth? (various answers: 6000 years and 4.56 billion years)
- What orbits around the Earth? (moon)
- How was the Earth created? (various answers: Big Bang Theory, God spoke it into existence, or other theories)
- How long have people been on Earth? (various answers)

Allow a bit of debate and discussion on this. After a couple of minutes, say: Sounds like there are lots of discrepancies with some of these answers. Some things we learn are pretty simple and straight forward, but others aren't so easy. It can make it seem hard to reconcile your faith and your reason.

Explain that as they get older, more and more of their beliefs may be challenged. In fact, some of them may have already encountered other people who would want to make them feel like they have to choose between being a Christian and being intelligent.

Say: Regardless of what other people may say, you don't have to choose between being intelligent and having a strong faith. Once an atheist, C.S. Lewis eventually realized that faith in God was indeed the most intelligent and reasonable conclusion to life's toughest questions.

LISTEN UP (20 minutes)
Review highlights from the life of C.S. Lewis from the background information above. Make sure to include aspects of his life that could mirror events from students' own lives, such as the death of a parent, school difficulties, physical limitations, war, etc.

Also spend some time on how intelligent and inquisitive C.S. Lewis was. The YouTube video "Religion and Science by C.S. Lewis Doodle" (https://www.youtube.com/watch?v=AJuOoYvi-cY) may be shown in part or in whole to illustrate just how brilliant of a debater Lewis was.

Finally, point out the impact Lewis' friendships had on his coming to faith.

Read Proverbs 13:20.
Walk with the wise and become wise,
For a companion of fools suffers harm.

Have students share how they think this verse applies to the life and experiences of C.S. Lewis. Then ask students if they believe it could apply to their own lives. Have a few share their thoughts.

NOW WHAT? (15 minutes)
Activity: Mark out a small obstacle course on the floor with the tape/rope. Make sure there are some turns and some obstacles, but nothing too difficult. Blindfold a student and have him/her try to complete the course. The other students should be around the course calling out to try to mislead the blindfolded student. They can also add/move some of the obstacles. Designate one of the students on the sides to be the "friend" who will try to help, rather than distract, the blindfolded person.

Repeat until all students who want to have had a chance to complete the course.

Ask: How hard was it to complete the course without being able to see? Was it hard to know who to trust and who to ignore? How important was it to have a friend you could trust to be able to guide you through?

Explain that although Lewis was their age over 100 years ago and he is regarded as a Christian superstar today, the important role his friends played in the development of his faith is very similar to that.

Allow time for discussion after each question.

Ask: What are some significant factors in your life that might impact your faith and understanding?

Ask: If your faith is ever challenged, do you think you would have an intelligent argument for why you stand on your faith? Have you ever considered why you believe what you believe?

Ask: Do the friends you have encourage you in your faith? Do you have friends that are not supportive of your faith?

LIVE IT (5 minutes)
Reassure students that it is okay to ask tough questions about why we believe what we believe. Encourage them to talk about those things with their pastor, youth pastor, parents, or other church leaders.

Issue a challenge to be an extraordinary Christian by being an encouraging friend like Tolkien and Dyson were to Lewis. Finally, close with this or a similar prayer: Creator God, we thank you for everything that is part of our world today. While there are things that are so incredible we may never be able to fully explain or comprehend them, we can rest assured that you have always been in control. Thank you, God, for your awesome ways that are still so much a mystery to us. Thank you for our friends who challenge and encourage us, both causing us to grow in our faith.

JUST IN CASE
Some of your students may have seen quotes attributed to Lewis on social media. He's also quoted by many Christian authors and preachers. But not all of these quotes are accurate. Some of them are paraphrases mistaken for quotes. Some of them are edited for clarity and effect but still keep the basic idea intact. At least one rather popular, supposed Lewis quote is absolutely inaccurate: "You do not have a soul. You are a soul. You have a body." Lewis' writings and lectures make it clear that he believed each human is comprised of body (flesh and bone), mind (will, personality, reason, etc.), and spirit (the God-implanted part that separates us from animals and allows us to commune with God, often called the soul), and that all three must be present for one to be a human being. Lewis further believed that all three of these continue after death; Lewis, basic Christian theology, and the "I believe in the resurrection of the body" of the Apostles' Creed all agree that it's not just the soul leaving the body and going to heaven, which is what this misquote seems to say.

DIGGING DEEPER
Some of Lewis' books are great for teens.

A Grief Observed was written after Lewis' wife's death. In it, he reflects on the process of grief. This is good to read when dealing with the loss of any loved one.

God in the Dock is a collection of essays on theology and ethics.

On Stories and Of Other Worlds are great reads for anyone who likes to write.

Out of the Silent Planet, Perelandra, and *That Hideous Strength* are a science fiction trilogy.

Surprised by Joy is Lewis' autobiography. Good biographies are *Jack* by George Sayer, *The Most Reluctant Convert* by David Downing, and *The Spiritual Legacy of C. S. Lewis* by Terry Glaspey. (Don't bother with *C. S. Lewis: A Biography* by A. N. Wilson.)

The Chronicles of Narnia is a series of seven novels. These are marketed as children's books, but brush aside that narrow marketing demographic and read them. If you read them as a child, re-read them and see what you notice now that you're older.

The Great Divorce isn't about a bad marriage ending, but rather the difference between heaven and hell (playing on the poem "The Marriage of Heaven and Hell" by William Blake). This novel explains heaven and hell better than any theological dissertation or "I died and saw a white light" memoir.

The Screwtape Letters is an entertaining and extremely challenging collection of fictional letters from a senior devil, Screwtape, instructing a junior devil, Wormwood, on how to keep Wormwood's human "patient" from becoming an effective Christian.

If you like movies, two have been made of Lewis' life, both titled "Shadowlands." The 1985 BBC version is more accurate; the 1993 version with Anthony Hopkins is more dramatic, but understates the Christianity.

NOTES

Resources used in compiling the background information: "Answers to Questions on Christianity" in God in the Dock by C. S. Lewis, dictionary.com, Jack by George Sayer, Lenten Lands by Douglas Gresham, Mere Christianity by C. S. Lewis, Surprised by Joy by C. S. Lewis. Photos used: "C.S Lewis" - http://goo.gl/2xyjF8, "Brain page 368" by Sue Clark - https://goo.gl/zStg4x.

FAITH OUT LOUD

ST. FRANCIS OF ASSISI
BY WHITNEY BROWN AND ANDY McCLUNG

SCRIPTURE
PSALM 24:1, MATTHEW 10:7-10, ACTS 20:35, LUKE 12:15, PHILIPPIANS 4:19, 1 TIMOTHY 6:10

THEME
The most important things in life aren't things.

LEADER INSIGHT

CONNECTING TO YOUR STUDENTS
Your students are probably quite materialistic (as we all are), even if they claim otherwise. At the very least, they want money for cars, for fuel, for clothes, for hobbies, for dating. Those who say money isn't very important to them probably either have plenty of it, or are ignorant about economics. In fact, they probably have an unhealthy relationship with money and material things...but don't even know it.

Encountering St. Francis and his life can help to change their perspective and outlook on material possessions.

Your students may already know something about St. Francis. The quote, "Preach the gospel at all times, and, when necessary, use words," is said to be his. They may have seen his statue—he's the one with small animals on him—in somebody's garden. They may also be familiar with the Franciscan prayer that begins, "Lord, make me an instrument of your peace..." If so, draw on this familiarity in teaching the lesson.

EXPLAINING THE TOPIC
Giovanni Bernadoni was born in Assisi, Italy, in 1181 or 1182, to a wealthy family. His father, a cloth merchant, loved all things French (including his French wife) and nicknamed Giovani "Francesco" (or "Francis" in English, which means "little Frenchman"). The nickname prevailed. Francis enjoyed being a rich kid and took full advantage of his family's wealth. He wanted to become a knight and gain fame for military victories. At the time, when most people were just trying to survive day to day, such dreams were limited to the rich. He did see military action, but it wasn't as glorious as he expected. He spent a year as a prisoner of war. This, and a long illness, changed his attitude. He turned his back on warfare and turned his heart toward the Christian faith of his parents, albeit gradually.

One day, probably in 1206 or 1207, while praying in the ruins of a church building near his home, Francis heard the crucifix say, "Francis, go and repair my house, which you see is falling down." Francis sold a bunch of his father's cloth, used the money to buy stones, and repaired the church building. This greatly angered his father. In response, Francis spent the next two years dressed humbly, wandering around the city giving away money and helping the poor, repairing church buildings, and enjoying the beauty of nature. When people recognized Francis and noticed how joyful he was, even though he was living like a beggar while he still had access to plenty of money, they asked him why he was so happy. He replied by saying that he had gotten married... to poverty. Francis' father eventually took legal action to cut Francis off from the family money. Francis' response this time was to renounce all wealth and fully embrace poverty. He gave the clothes he was wearing to his father and, naked, walked out of the city to live in nature.

At a church service in 1208 or 1209, someone read Matthew 10:7-10, and Francis realized that embracing poverty for himself wasn't enough; he had to tell others about the joy of voluntary poverty. He left the wilderness and returned to the cities, where he helped the poor and preached to those not living in poverty. He dressed in the least comfortable clothes he could find and survived on whatever food people gave him. Francis had come to understand that by voluntarily becoming poor, he could both draw closer to Jesus, who was poor, and understand the life of the impoverished, whom he was called to help.

Amazingly, people were drawn to Francis and wanted to adopt his way of life. When he had eleven followers, he petitioned the pope for official recognition. The pope hesitated until he had a dream in which he saw Francis, alone, physically holding up one of the great cathedrals of Rome as it was falling over. The pope granted the request and the Order of Friars Minor (the lesser/humbler brothers) became an official order of the Roman Catholic Church.

The order, guided by some simple rules Francis drew from scripture (including taking nothing when they traveled and giving up all personal possessions), imitated Jesus by denying worldly wealth, living in voluntary poverty, wandering about while preaching repentance, helping peasants do their work, and taking care of the sick and outcast.

After the order grew to include thousands of men, it necessarily became more structured and institutional. Francis worked hard to keep this success from changing the founding rules.

Francis also helped establish an order for women, the Order of St. Clare, and an order for persons of both genders who couldn't fully commit to a life of poverty and itinerancy, called the Third Order of St. Francis. Francis stepped down from leadership in 1220 and mostly withdrew from public life. He spent his last few years praying, meditating, finding peace in nature, and writing. This is when he wrote about caring for animals, something for which he is well known. After a long period of prayer in 1224, Francis manifested the stigmata, which means he was so close to Christ spiritually that his body miraculously developed the same wounds Jesus received on the cross. In 1226 Francis died in a simple hut. He was made a saint just two years later.

A famous quote attributed to St. Francis is: "Start by doing what is necessary, then what is possible, and suddenly you are doing the impossible." Francis started by paying more attention to the poor than to money (what was necessary), then he walked away from material possessions altogether (what was possible), and now dozens of ministry organizations have been established, hundreds of schools and hospitals have been built, and millions of acts of ministry have been done as a result of this one man responding to God (the impossible).

THEOLOGICAL UNDERPINNINGS

St. Francis didn't own a car, of course, but if he did, it'd probably have one of those bumper stickers that read, "The most important things in life aren't things." God gradually revealed to Francis that money isn't everything, that imitating Jesus by denying oneself material pleasures and caring for the poor is what it means to be Christ-like. Francis knew what kind of person wealth had made him. He also knew, from scripture, what kind of person Jesus was. And he saw the huge difference between the two. God seems to know when we can handle a huge revelation all at once, and when we need to receive it in stages. None of those steps, however, ever seem to be easy enough to be called "baby steps." They each take a difficult leap of faith. Apparently, God follows the logic of "if it's easy, it ain't worth much."

Money (or, at least, some form of currency) is necessary to survive, and the Bible never says money itself is bad, or having a lot of money is bad. The Bible does, however, say a lot about having a right relationship with money. Jesus said we should treasure only the things that truly matter, not material things (Matthew 6:19-20, Luke 12:13-21), and that being rich makes it really hard to live the kind of life that leads to heaven (Matthew 19:24). Paul said that loving money leads to all kinds of evil (1 Timothy 6:10). Plenty of scriptures warn against greed.

Many pastors today regularly remind their congregations that ministry takes money. Francis might have disagreed, saying that the only thing necessary for ministry to take place is the desire to be like Jesus.

APPLYING THE LESSON TO YOUR OWN LIFE

Grab a pad and pen. Make a list of everything you own or possess. (This could take a while!)
What was your relationship with money/material things like when you were your students' age? What could someone have said or done to improve it? How healthy is your relationship with money/material things now? Where did you draw your criteria from to determine the health of your current relationship?

What material things do you own right now that you could you give away and never miss? What would you be willing to give up? Who could use those things?

Do you own your possessions, or do your possessions own you? If you, like Francis, felt God calling you to walk away from all material possessions, could you?

What do you do, on a regular basis, to help the poor? How do you feel about helping the poor being a basic Christian practice? Recall a time you helped someone with a serious material/financial need. Recall a time someone helped you with a serious material/financial need. Which felt better, giving or receiving?

ST. FRANCIS OF ASSISI
BY WHITNEY BROWN AND ANDY McCLUNG

SCRIPTURE
PSALM 24:1, MATTHEW 10:7-10, ACTS 20:35, LUKE 12:15, PHILIPPIANS 4:19, 1 TIMOTHY 6:10

LEADER PREP

RESOURCE LIST
- A dry erase board or a large piece of paper/poster board
- Markers for whatever you choose to write on
- Small pieces of paper (enough for each student to have 3-5)
- Various colors of crayons, unwrapped so the sides can be used.

BEFORE THE LESSON
On the board or large paper, write the following Bible verse groupings with enough space underneath each section for a short summary of the passage:

Verses	13-15	16-21
	22-28	29-31
	32-34	

GET STARTED

CALL TO WORSHIP
Read the following prayer responsively as a Call to Worship.
(Alternate Idea: Instead of a responsive reading with one person leading and all others responding, go around the room with each student speaking one line until the prayer is complete.)

The Peace Prayer by St. Francis
Leader: Lord, make me an instrument of Thy peace;
All: Where there is hatred, let me sow love;
Leader: Where there is injury, pardon;
All: Where there is error, the truth;
Leader: Where there is doubt, the faith;
All: Where there is despair, hope;
Leader: Where there is darkness, light;
All: And where there is sadness, joy.
Leader: O Divine Master,
Grant that I may not so much seek
All: To be consoled, as to console;
Leader: To be understood, as to understand;
All: To be loved as to love.

Leader: For it is in giving that we receive;
All: It is in pardoning that we are pardoned;
Leader: And it is in dying that we are born to eternal life.
All: Amen.

CALL TO WAKE UP
Lead your students in a variation of the game, "I'm Going on a Trip." Tell them the following:

You're going on a trip and can only take what you can carry. You do not know where you will stay. You do not have any cash, checks, or credit cards. Given this scenario, we're going to take turns going around the room playing "I'm Going on a Trip," and take turns listing what we will take. The first person will say, "I'm going on a trip, and I'm taking... (something that begins with the letter A)." The next person will say, "I'm going on a trip, and I'm taking... (something that begins with the letter B)." This continues all the way through the alphabet.

(Variation: Instead of going through the entire alphabet, have the first student name what they will bring (anything that meets the criteria listed). The second person repeats the first person's item and adds their own. The third person lists the first and second persons' items and then adds their own, and so on until everyone has added their item.)

Conduct an Internet search of images of St. Francis of Assisi
to show your students different depictions of him.

LISTEN UP

LISTEN UP (20-25 minutes)
Read from the "Explaining the Topic" section of the "Leader's Insights" to share St. Francis' biography with your students.

Luke 12:13-34

13Someone in the crowd said to him, "Teacher, tell my brother to divide the family inheritance with me." 14But he said to him, "Friend, who set me to be a judge or arbitrator over you?" 15And he said to them, "Take care! Be on your guard against all kinds of greed; for one's life does not consist in the abundance of possessions." 16Then he told them a parable: "The land of a rich man produced abundantly. 17And he thought to himself, 'What should I do, for I have no place to store my crops?' 18Then he said, 'I will do this: I will pull down my barns and build larger ones, and there I will store all my grain and my goods. 19And I will say to my soul, Soul, you have ample goods laid up for many years; relax, eat, drink, be merry.' 20But God said to him, 'You fool! This very night your life is being demanded of you. And the things you have prepared, whose will they be?' 21So it is with those who store up treasures for themselves but are not rich towards God."

22He said to his disciples, "Therefore I tell you, do not worry about your life, what you will eat, or about your body, what you will wear. 23For life is more than food, and the body more than clothing. 24Consider the ravens: they neither sow nor reap, they have neither storehouse nor barn, and yet God feeds them. Of how much more value are you than the birds! 25And can any of you by worrying add a single hour to your span of life? 26If then you are not able to do so small a thing as that, why do you worry about the rest? 27Consider the lilies, how they grow: they neither toil nor spin; yet I tell you, even Solomon in all his glory was not clothed like one of these. 28But if God so clothes the grass of the field, which is alive today and tomorrow is thrown into the oven, how much more will he clothe you—you of little faith! 29And do not keep striving for what you are to eat and what you are to drink, and do not keep worrying. 30For it is the nations of the world that strive after all these things, and your Father knows that you need them. 31Instead, strive for his kingdom, and these things will be given to you as well.

32"Do not be afraid, little flock, for it is your Father's good pleasure to give you the kingdom. 33Sell your possessions, and give alms. Make purses for yourselves that do not wear out, an unfailing treasure in heaven, where no thief comes near and no moth destroys. 34For where your treasure is, there your heart will be also."

Say: Read the passage again, and pause at the following verses to create an outline/summary of what is happening in each section.

Verses	13-15	16-21
	22-28	29-31
	32-34	

Using the board or poster you have prepared with the divided verses, have them write out their summaries for each section.

Ask: This passage began with a man asking for his share of his family's inheritance, transitioned into a parable, and ended with Jesus telling his followers not to worry. How are all these things connected?

Ask: What in this passage relates to your life?

Ask: How does the life of St. Francis live out what Jesus told his followers in this passage?

DISCUSSION QUESTIONS

NOW WHAT

NOW WHAT? (10-15 minutes)
By living in poverty, St. Francis had a very close connection with creation. He cared greatly for plants and animals. As you continue the lesson, go outside. Take the paper and unwrapped crayons with you.

Tell your students to explore the natural area around them in silence, considering what they have heard and learned so far today. As they explore, they can make texture rubbings of things they find in nature (leaves, tree bark, etc.). This is done by placing the paper over the texture and rubbing over the paper with the side of the unwrapped crayon. Ask them not to damage the plants when doing this activity.

When they return from their time of silence, invite your students to write their own "Peace Prayer" like the one they read at the beginning of the lesson by St. Francis. What does peace mean to them? Where do they find peace in their lives? Where do they need it? This can be done as a group or individually, and could even be written over their favorite texture rubbing.

LIVE IT

LIVE IT (5-10 minutes)
In closing, ask your students to consider the way St. Francis lived and what Jesus told his followers in the text they studied today. Ask them to think about these questions:

What material things do you own right now that you could you give away and never miss? What would you be willing to give up? Who could use those things?

They can share together or think to themselves as they answer these questions. Challenge them to come up with an action plan to implement as soon as they return home, in order to gather those items and give them to the people or places that can use them. Remind them to ask their parents' permission before giving away something that wasn't theirs to give away.

DIGGING DEEPER

Here are some of the original rules Francis wrote for the order:

• They were to live in obedience and chastity, "without property, and to follow in the doctrine and footsteps of our Lord Jesus Christ."

• In whatever places they were "among others to serve or to work," they were not be in charge of anyone else, but be "inferior and subject to all who are in the same house."

• They could each have "one tunic with a hood, and another without a hood," if they really needed the second one, "and a cord and breeches."

• They could not "carry or receive money or coin in any manner, or cause it to be received, either for clothing, or for books, or as the price of any labor, or indeed for any reason," except to help care for sick brothers. They could, however, beg for money to buy food and such, but only from believers, and only because it is part of a Christian's duty to help the poor. Begging was an act of humility.

• When traveling, they were to carry "neither bag, nor purse, nor bread, nor money, nor a staff," which means they only lodged where invited and only ate what was offered them.

• They also maintained a daily regimen of prayers and worship.

JUST IN CASE

If a student asks if Francis was really completely opposed to wealth, tell this story. When one friar returned from doing ministry, he was elated because someone had given him a gold coin. Francis told the friar to hold the coin in his teeth and bury it in a pile of manure. That, said Francis, is the best place for gold. In his original rules, he wrote, "we ought not to have more use and esteem of money and coin than of stones... if we should chance to find money in any place, let us no more regard it than the dust we tread under our feet."

NOTES

Resources used in compiling background material: A History of the Christian Church by Williston Walkerl, sacred-texts.com, The Story of Christianity Vol. I, by Justo Gonzalez. Photos used: "Master of the bardi saint francis . St. Francis and scenes from his life 13 cent Santa croce" by by Master of San Francesco Bardi – wikimedia - https://goo.gl/y0nXxZ, "$900 Cash" by Alexi Kostibas - https://goo.gl/zStg4x

www.ingramcontent.com/pod-product-compliance
Lightning Source LLC
Chambersburg PA
CBHW041427090426
42741CB00002B/62